THE VALUES OF THE ANTHEMS AND THE PLEDGE TO NIGERIA

Comparative Studies Of The Old And The New
National Anthems With The Pledge In Relation
To The Nigerian Value System

I0115235

Dipo Toby Alakija

CALVARY ROCK Resources

ISBN: 978-978-498-7400
978-4987406
Printed in United States

Published by
CALVARY ROCK PUBLISHING

19, Ajina Street, Ikenne Remo,
Ogun State,
Nigeria.

In Conjunction With
CHRISTIAN EDUCATION AND MINISTRATION SERVICES (CEMS)

ACKNOWLEDGMENTS

I must first acknowledge the encouragement we got from various State Ministries Of Education in Nigeria and the Universal Basic Education Board in each State after going through this book and other books titled: "The Values Of The National Anthem And The Pledge To Nigeria," "Building Your Future And The Nation Now" and "Bloodshed In Campus", which is the result of our research works into social vices with particular focus on campus secret cults. All the books, including "The Young Nigerian Story Book" which are approved by these Ministries as subject books in the States are designed to curb the social vices in the society and to be used to build young ones and adults into patriotic citizens of Nigeria. The Federal Ministry Of Education and all the State Ministries Of Education (SMoE) that have encouraged us with the responses are appreciated for their supports.

Secondly, I appreciate the CEMS Project Director, Pastor Samuel A. Ilori who toured round about 30 States in Nigeria to present the books to Commissioners for education and explain the expected results of using the books in the States.

The resource team members of Calvary Rock Publishing And Christian Education And Ministrations Services like Rev. Abayomi O. Solesi, Mrs Omolade Martha Alakija, Pastor Abiodun Adekunle, Evang. Juwon Sokoya, Toluwanimi Margaret Alakija, Lekan Somule, Jonathan Ayeri, Faith Iyanuni Alakija, Juliana Oluwaseun Ekundayo, Blessing Alakija and a host of others are really appreciated.

With the help of God and these people, this book is designed to help Nigerian children to appreciate the meaning of the National Anthem and understand the implication of breaking the pledges they make to the Nation.

With the efforts of our team to package this book, it is our hope that it will influence children who are the leaders of tomorrow to be responsible and valuable in the society.

Dedication

This book is dedicated to all Nigerian parents who are doing all they can to groom their children into reasonable and responsible citizens of Nigeria either within and outside the country.

INTRODUCTION OF NIGERIAN VALUE SYSTEM

A close studies and comparison of the old, new national anthems and the pledge of Nigeria will reveal the fame work of the National Value System. This frame work which is expected to be built upon by everybody in the positions of leaders, teachers and parents are neglected. The neglect of this frame work is what brings about chaos, vices and crimes in our organized society. As indicated in the author's article titled: Patriotism and Moral Issues, there was a time in Nigeria when the people were ready to bake the national cake for the good of old, young and future generations with everyone getting his or her fair share. Mice soon find their ways to the national store house which is the national treasury through either armed-forces or other means, eating and destroying the means of the national cake - the infrastructures to build the economy of the nation. Before anyone knew it, most people have developed unpatriotic attitudes of eating out the national cake instead of labouring to bake it. When the national cake was barely enough even for the mice to consume; people began to find any means to survive, including killing one another for money or rituals to get wealth. The problem in Nigeria now is not the mice that caused the problem but the unpatriotic attitudes which most Nigerians have developed in other to survive or to cushion the effect of their sufferings or hunger.

Based on some findings, it is save to conclude that the problems of Nigeria are Nigerians, especially those who have eroded the frame work of the National Value System. To rebuild this frame work, the values of both the National Anthems and The Pledge To Nigeria, which are going to be studied critically must be appreciated and understood as part of the law by all Nigerian, especially the youths - the future of the nation. Without the need to recall history, the focus must be on the subject of the National Anthems and The Pledge To Nigeria and what are meant to be taught or achieved through them.

THE OLD NATION ANTHEM OF NIGERIA

The old nation anthem was used from independence in 1960 until it was changed to the new one in 1978. The lyrics was composed by Lillian Jean Willians, a British expatriate. The melody was composed by Frances Berda and adopted in October 1, 1960. The old national anthem goes this way:

> Nigeria we hail thee,
> Our own dear native land,
> Though tribe and tongue may differ
> In brotherhood we stand,
> Nigerians all, and proud to serve
> Our sovereign mother land.
>
> Our flag shall be a symbol
> That truth and justice reign,
> In peace or battle honour'd,
> And this we count as gain
> To hand on to our children.
> A banner without stain
>
> Oh God of all creations
> Grant this our one request
> Help us to build a nation
> Where no man is oppressed,
> And so with peace and plenty
> Nigeria maybe blessed

Going by the analysis of the old national anthem, Lillian seemed to have studied the diversities of Nigerian cultures, norms, traditional and family values properly. He was able to weave them into a national anthem.

ANALYSIS OF THE OLD NATIONAL ANTHEM

Nigeria We Hail Thee: This sounds like a poetic or literary way of giving praise to or an act of calling the attention of someone who is very special and honourable. Nigerians, just like other countries that exist today, are those who make existence of the nation of Nigeria possible. This is later recognized in the descriptions of the tribes and tongues that differ. In other words, Nigerians are made to see themselves as special people, irrespective of their differences. This is vital to note before they can be proud of whom they are.

Our Own Dear Native Land: This is the recognition of all the areas in the Eastern, Western, Southern and Northern parts of

5

the nation as the native land of all Nigerians as it reflects in the constitution. Thus they have the rights to live in any part of the country without feeling like strangers.

<u>Though Tribe And Tongue May Differ, In Brotherhood We Stand</u>: This is description of the fact that though there are different tribes and languages in the native land of all Nigerians but they are made to see themselves as brothers simply because they are of the same citizenship and purposes. Thus they have to stand together as brothers without dwelling on the differences in their tribes and languages.

<u>Nigerians All, And Proud To Serve Our Sovereign Motherland</u>: You will note the use of motherland, which is different from the new anthem that describes Nigeria as "fatherland" but what is common to both is the service to the nation. The reason the fatherland is more suitable is that the name of a family is always derived from the name of the father. Thus the name of the fatherland of all Nigerians wherever they are in the world is Nigeria . The major thing to note here is serving the nation with pride. The aspect of service to Nigeria will be explained later.

<u>Our Flag Shall Be A Symbol</u>: The design of the national flag by Michael Taiwo Akinkunmi (a retired civil servant, born on 10th May 1936) depicts who Nigerians and what the nation is expected to be.

The national flag was designed in 1959 and was officially adopted on the independence day in October 1st 1960. The green, white and green colour symbolize two different things. The white stripe symbolizes peace and unity in the country as it reflects in the two anthems and the pledge to Nigeria while the green symbolizes fertile land, which is of one, if not the major sources of the country's wealth. Although the old national anthem may not explicitly indicate all the symbols in the flag but the next lines indicate peace that may be brought about by truth and justice. Thus the flag, according to this line, symbolizes that the united and peaceful Nigerians dwell in their

Pa Michael Taiwo Akinkunmi Who Designed The Flag Of Nigeria

6

fertile fatherland.

That Truth And Justice Reign: Through this line and that of the new anthem, truth and justice are meant to characterize everything about Nigeria for the following reasons:

(i) Without truth, there would be miscarriage of justice.

(ii) Without truth, criminals will appear innocent while innocent people may look like criminals.

(iii) Without truth, leaders would deceive the followers.

(iv) Without truth, especially about the state of the nation either economically or politically or in other things, the country cannot move forward at all.

(v) Without truth, leaders and citizens will be misinformed, making the country to be deformed.

In Peace Or battle Honoured: This line further emphasizes the need for truth and justice to reign. This line seems to indicate that a battle may need to be fought with honour before there can be peace. Or in order to maintain peace, there may be battle to be fought with honour. This battle may not necessarily mean war but struggle to preserve lives and properties or tussles with leaders that abuse their positions, war against political oppressions or economic depressions. Unknown to many Nigerians, lack of truth like declaration of assets of politicians before

Nigerian Soldiers Go Into Battle With Boko Haram Below

assuming offices or manipulations of electoral results are injustices that can create rooms for crimes and vices. If Nigerians are made conscious of the need for truth and justice; educating them about their rights, they would be better equipped to wage war against crimes and vices instead of getting involved

7

in any of them.

<u>And These We Count As Gain</u>: The peace and the honour that may be achieved in battle as a result of the prevail of truth and justice in the nation are counted as gain. This line emphasizes the fact that other gains, including financial benefits will soon vanish if peace and honour are not achieved. The reason is that crimes and vices which are threats to lives and properties are expensive to fight. If, however, the truth about a citizen or a situation is discovered, justice must be done to safeguard the interests of the nation. To illustrate this, I would like to quote from one of my papers that compares the nation as human body with many parts (citizens.) If the body is infected with deadly bacteria (crimes and vices) that threaten the entire system, antidotes (truth and justice) must be applied to save the whole body (the system) from breaking down or getting destroyed. In other words, natural resources or things that bring wealth are not the real wealth of a nation. Real wealth is the peace and honour that reign in the nation. Since the citizens are the ones that bring about peace, they must be made to live in peace by abiding by the law. Justice enforces the law and order in the society. The essence of locking up criminals in prison is not just to punish them but to serve as deterrent to others. In a situation where a criminal is allowed to go away with the crime he has committed, the peace of the nation would be under threat because others maybe encouraged to commit crimes. The government would be forced to spend the gain in the natural and other resources so as to secure lives and properties. For this reason, the real gain is not the financial benefit but the peace and the honour that are achieved while applying truth and justice.

<u>To Hand On Our Children</u>: This line recognizes the fact that children are the future of every nation. The followings prove this to be so:

(i) Children will grow into adults who would later become parents or grand or great parent as years roll by.

(ii) Whatever children of today learn are what will design their lives years later. For this reason, they are and

Students During Independence Day On October 1st 1960

8

must be compelled by parents or Governments to go to school and learn to be useful and productive in future. Otherwise, they will constitute nuisances like street beggars.

(iii) If children learn wrong thing now, it will become very difficult if not impossible to change when they grow up with it. According to the results of series of research works of the author and that of others that are

Nigerian School Children During One Of The Recent Independent Day Celebrations, Holding Nigerian Flag.

compiled in the book titled "The Insanity Of Humanity," most children who are raised and taught through network of televisions are intellectually dead in their early teens.

The line also implies the legacies that are to be handed over to children, which they will also hand order to their own children. If at any point, bad legacies are handed over to them, they will also hand the same to their children with the bad effect on the nation.

A Banner Without Stain: This line talks about the good legacies which are to be handed over to the children. A lot of legacies (banners) that are stained (bad) had been given to the present generation which is taking their tolls on the nation. These legacies include though not limited to:

(I) *Religious Sentiments*: Religion is good only when it promotes peace or adds moral value to the people or enhance the National Value. However, any religion that is enforced either by coercion or manipulation is a violation of fundamental human right as guarantied by the constitution and the gift of freewill that is given by God. The end result is rebellion that may lead to the breakdown of law and order, which is enough to threaten the peace of the nation. Because Nigeria is a secular state, religion can only be offered and accepted or rejected by

A Civil Unrest Scene That Led To Deaths Of Many People In Nigeria.

9

reasons and logics as perceived by the person to receive it. If it is offered and accepted through this way, this can bring respect to principles of the religion. Thus any religion that encourages violence or bloodshed is a crime. When people become sentimental about a religion to the extent of breaking the law, the children would be offered bad legacy. They are forced to either join the religious oppressors or fight against them. In either case, the end result is violence.

(ii) _Fraudulent Practice_: This is a dirty or terrible legacy that is common in every section within the system of Nigeria, ranging from politics; civil service; economic; social and academic to religious and other institutions and organizations or establishments. You will note from the issue of the national cake at the introduction of this subject that the "mice" introduced fraudulent practice, which made the people to develop unpatriotic attitudes. The attitudes of Nigerians are described as bacteria in the body system (national value system). The bacteria indicate their existence in the body (the society) through rampant vices and crimes. The end result of all these is either the governments spend the fortune of the nation fighting crimes and building more prisons that will accommodate more criminals, doing all it can to secure lives and properties or rebuild the nation through young ones. None of these is an easy may out but the most effective method is to combine the two. In essence, it is deadly to hand over stained (bad) banner (legacy) to young ones.

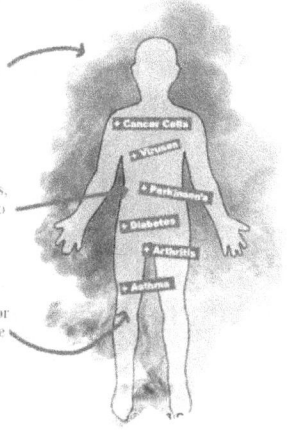

HOW DISEASE OCCURS

1. Outside NEGATIVE ENERGY force surrounds the body. (Represented by black smoke for illustration purpose only)

2. Negative energy creates Cancer cells, viruses, or other dreadful diseases to the victim's body.

3. Disease remains as long as its creator (negative energy) is surrounding the body.

(iii) _Antisocial Behaviours_: This is also a stain in the banner (destructive legacy). Nigerians are good at giving good and sound speeches but most do not follow what they say. Many politicians make lofty promises that influence the people to vote for them but when they get into the office, they care only for themselves. Parents at times teach their children good conduct but they themselves misbehave in their presence, making them confused. Teachers teach their students the right thing but they do the wrong thing. Vast majority of Nigerians do not care about saying or doing the right thing at all. Some artists in the bid to be recognized in the society and to make money produce music and movies that corrupt the society, making antisocial behaviour seems like a normal way of life. Most people, including some political and religious leaders do not take cognizance of the fact antisocial behaviours, which at times begin from homes and schools always spread across the nation through means of entertainment, information, communication and even education. Safeguarding these channels of evils at this level in the society is getting much more difficult.

Oh God Of All Creation: This is the first line of the third stanza of the old national anthem. If this is compared with the first line of the second stanza of the new anthem, you will note that it is made official that Nigeria as a nation believes in God right from the onset. It appears Nigerian forefathers understood the roles the belief in God plays in the lives of the people or in molding their ways of life in a positive manner.

From various research works, the following reasons make it necessary for people to believe there is God:

(i) Without belief in God, a Godless society can be created. Because God is perceive as creator of all things including mankind, he has the power to also kill or to destroy. When people are conscious of this, it makes them feel accountable before God when they die. If this consciousness of accountability before God is removed from people, they can become dangerous unless the law is forceful enough to make them behave right. Even then, because the law does not have the enforcement agents in every nook and cranny of the society, the people can still commit crimes and get away with them. But with consciousness that God is everywhere, seeing everything and having all information,

11

the people tend to behave right. So the belief in God which the two anthems introduced is not really intended to make the people so fanatical to the extent of killing others in the name of any religion but to make them know that there is God watching everything everybody does either in secret or in the open.

(ii) The belief in God can boost people's moral values. Vladimir Lenin, a Russian dictator who can be considered as the of cause of the deaths of millions of his people said, *"there are no moral in politics; there is only experience. A scoundrel maybe used to us just because he is a scoundrel."* He also added, *"Give me four years to teach the children and the seed I have sown will never be uprooted."* And he also indicated that the best revolutionists are youths devoid of morals. When you consider his method of ruling Russia you will observe that he first removed every form of belief in God that always boost the people's moral values. When the youths who are always full of energy, going by his theory and activities, were devoid of morals, he would train and use them to eliminate anyone that tried to oppose him or his policies. This method is similar to most other dictators all over the world. The belief in God thus plays vital role in formation of good conduct and positive attitudes of the people. Any religion that cannot achieve this is not to be encouraged in anyway.

(iii) The belief in God makes a person committed to one another as a members of the society or the fatherland.

Grant This Our One Request: The belief in God assures the people that if they pray to him, he will answer them. If their request is granted, it increases their faith in God. If not, it would be assumed that their faith is not strong enough. In whichever way it goes, people; especially young ones are to be taught of the need to talk to God in prayer. The followings are what place values on prayers:

(i) Prayers are always believed to be answered when there is divine intervention as we have seen miracles happening in this country.

(ii) Prayers are perceived to have been answered when the people are given directions on how to solve some problems

like the case of Ebola crisis, which a Nigerian physician called Ameyo Adadevoh stopped from spreading in Nigeria. She detained a Liberian called Patrick Sawyer who was probably sent to spread the virus to kill Nigerians, going by the way he was eager to leave the hospital. Adadevoh died on 19 August 2014 of the disease which she stopped from spreading.

Dr. Ameyo Adadevoh

(iii) Prayers are also believed to be answered when people get ideas on how to increase the wealth of the nation, make life comfortable for the people and or capture the undesirable elements that use diabolical means to terrorize members of the society or community.

(iv) Prayers are also valuable because it can positively shape the psyche of the people through the feelings that if they are to get God involved in anything, they have to live and behave right. This is observed when some Christians and Muslims are in their fasting and praying periods. Most of them always behave right at these periods.

Help Us To Build A Nation: Because of the belief in God and that he created all things, the people know that he can build the nation and make it beautiful and habitable where just as the next line indicates, no one is oppressed. If the belief that God is to build the nation exists in the people, it is also assumed that God is to inspire them to move the nation forward. This line of nation building is so crucial that it also reflects in the second stanza of the new anthem just as the line: Oh, God of Creation reflects in the two. This line, going by the analogy of the two anthems is crucial for the following reasons:

(I) God creates individuals for different purposes. His commitments to mankind makes him to provide all we need such as rain, air, sun and other things so as to stay alive and fulfil the purposes.

(ii) Just as God is committed to the people by ensuring that they enjoy life to its fullness, everybody is expected to be committed to him by taking good care of his creations, including human beings. Leaders must be committed to the followers by putting their interests into considerations while parents must put the interest of their children and their future ahead of theirs. Failure to do this will amount to misplacement of commitments, which can violate the law of orderliness of God, bringing about confusions; chaos and conflicts.

(iii) Individuals are also made to be committed to one another by being one another's keepers. All Nigerian children must be seen as the future of the nation. Thus they can be blessings or curses to the nation, depending on how they are raised. There were many occasions in Nigeria when parents failed in their responsibilities to their children who later grow into armed-robbers, kidnappers and other criminals that terrorize the nation. If all Nigerian adults do not see all Nigerian children as their future and are allowed to learn wrong things, they will grow into nuisances that terrorize the nation years later. Youths who do not fit into the value system are the ones in secret cults on campus, organizing or joining vice rings or group of criminals that pose threats to the peace of the nation in order to be relevant. This often results into their untimely deaths as it is observed nowadays.

Where No Man Is Oppressed: Again, this line is reflected in the new national anthem in the first stanza that reads: "one nation bound in freedom." The two indicate that if one is not free, he or she is oppressed.

Every oppressed person is a slave and the oppressor is the taskmaster. The oppression of any citizen in the society is the oppression of the nation. This line is to ensure that no one is oppressed and no oppressor is allowed. These are the consequences of any nation that is oppressed either by the leaders or by another country, going by historical facts:

(i) The Apartheid System Of Government in South Africa between 1948 and 1991, which was a racial segregation under the

The Oppressors And The Oppressed

rulership of white minority brought about oppression of the blacks. The result of that was constant violence and mass murder of blacks that are ready to die for their freedom. Thus any oppressed nation is bound to revolt one day.

The Oppressed Child Who Is Supposed To Be In School, Building His Future

(ii) Any oppressed nation would take steps towards regression instead of progression. Oppression of the people destroys their abilities to move the nation forward either economically, socially or politically.

(iii) Crimes and vices are always on the increase in any nation that is oppressed.

Child Oppressor Who Is Trained To Waste Human Lives

This is due to the fact that the value system, including family; moral and traditional values would have been eroded. For this reason, while raising youths that would be used to oppressed the people in future, Vladimir Lenin, the Russian dictator said, "the best revolutionists are youth devoid of morals."

Oppressive Government's Power In Action

Before considering what can result into the oppression of the nation, it is instructive to note that most people do not seem to care how a leader assume authority or leadership position as long as he or she meets up to their expectation. Thus what can result into oppressions of the people are as follows:

(i) Unpatriotic attitudes of leaders, especially the ones that failed to put the interests of the people ahead of his or hers. Such leaders include but not limited to political, religious, traditional and community leaders.

(ii) Ignorance of either the leaders or the followers or of both of them. A lot of people assume leadership positions without the slightest idea of how to lead. Apart from that, they lack information about the needs of the people they are leading. Thus they do not know how to meet these needs.

(iii) Selfishness or self interest which can be defined as lack of considerations for others motivates most people to contest for leadership positions. From observations, leaders who lack considerations for others always oppress the followers in order to get what they want.

(iv) Arrogance often times makes it hard for many people in authority to learn, especially from those who are more experienced than them. Arrogant leaders often do not care who is oppressed under their leadership. Arrogant people always feel that when they assume authority, they are above others. If anyone tries to challenge their authorities in any way, they tend to oppress the person with their powers.

The antidotes to oppressions of citizens by their leaders, especially political leaders are as follows:

(i) Although intelligence is not enough to make good leadership but it is one of the greatest hallmarks that characterizes good leaders. If intelligent people do not bid or contest for leadership positions, fools will find their ways there either for financial incentives or the prestige that goes along with them. If fools are in positions of power as Nigeria had experienced it over the years, every sector within the nation or organization or institution takes a nose dive into various levels of catastrophes, including political and economic disasters. The reason is that intelligent crooks will find it easy to use the fool in power to their advantages. In other words, the fool in power is an ideal tool in the hands of crooks to oppress the people.

(ii) Another thing that can be attributed to good leadership is good and positive attitudes of the leaders which can always be assessed through their reputations. A lot of Nigerians who are known as criminals often times assumed the positions of authorities. Many people erroneously believe that politics is a dirty game. Politics actually becomes dirty only if dirty people are allowed to make it dirty. It is through political activities that people elect their political leaders. If leaders are dirty, the society would be dirty. The question is:

if everywhere is dirty, who would be clean? In fact, no matter how clean a person may try to be, he would be made dirty if he goes into politics that had been made dirty by dirty people. Take for instance a State that owns it workers for well over a year simply because the Governor was dirty enough embezzle to the State fund. What should be expected in a State like that is for the filth to spread to every section in the State, starting from the Civil Service. This is what often leads to briberies, corruptions and other things that will work against the progress of the State. No matter how clean a person maybe, if he is confronted with a situation like this; he would be forced to bend or compromise his principles. Now people may wonder if it is possible to have a clean leader. It is possible if Uruguay can have a president like Jose Mujica since 2010. As at writing this book, he is considered the poorest but the best President in the world. What earned his position? He donates 90% of his salary to charity. When he felt sick, he waited in line in the public hospital before he could see the doctor. This man is actually teaching the world what clean politics and services to the nation are all about.

Uruguay President Jose Mujica Waited To See The Doctor In A Public Hospital When He Was Sick - A Good Example Of Good Leadership

(iii) Humility is not only part of good and positive attitude of a leader but also an outstanding virtue that characterizes good leadership in all walks of life; including politics, business, community, family and religion. This virtue makes a leader teachable, attentive and sympathetic to the plights of others. Many leaders seem to possess this virtue while vying for leadership positions but soon after they are elected, they become arrogant.

(iv) Firm leadership is also required to serve as antidote to oppression of the people. Being humble does not mean the leader should not take his stand when he or she has to. As it is in the nature of man to seek to control many things;

including what he lacks the ability to control, many people always attempt to control the leaders. Also most people in powers all over the world do not want to release powers to others even after another person had been elected or selected to lead. Leaders must strictly follow the law and order like the constitution that guides the society or the regulation that regulate the organization. Political leaders in powers are expected to exercise their constitutional authority to lead the nation even in the face of fierce oppositions without fear and without abusing their powers. A weak administration in any given country is vulnerable to corruption and compromise on principles of law, thereby exposing the citizens to oppression.

(v) The leaders must be disciplined because it takes disciplined leaders to discipline others. Without discipline in the society, lawlessness would be on the increase. Without force of the law, vices and crimes would be on the increase. Discipline increases productivity of labour and effectiveness of knowledge acquisition of students in schools.

(vi) Kindness and tolerance of the leadership and the citizens. It must be embedded in everybody of the need to make sacrifices for the good of the society and for others. Thus the people do not need to place price tag on everything they do for the good of others, especially those who cannot afford to pay for the services. Most Nigerians, as it is observed, are not ready to do anything good for free. They always find it hard to work without incentives. The case of National Youth Service Corps programme, where serving graduates would expect

Hardworking Nigerians Whose Patriotic Spirits Are Dampened By Some Unpatriotic Leaders

18

the Federal Government to pay for the services they render to the nation and at the same time expect the organization or institution or establishment to remunerate them for the same service. With this attitude, it becomes very hard if not impossible to do things that would be beneficial to others or the nation without the beneficiaries having to pay for them.

And So With People And Plenty: Again, you will note the similarity between this line of the old and the second stanza of the new anthems, which is "To Build A Nation Where Peace And Justice Shall Reign." This implies that the two anthems recognize the fact that "Where No Man Is Oppressed" as in old or when "One Nation Is Bound In Freedom" as in the new anthems, there would be enough to feed the present and the future citizens of the nation. Where people are "oppressed" or not "bound in freedom", however, there would be no peace in the society and there would be lack, according to the old anthem and "peace and justice" cannot

With People And Without Plenty Food, Citizens Will Seem Like Refugees In Their own Country.

reign, according to the new anthem. In other words, the followings are the results of peace in the society:

(i) There would be enough workforce of people who are not and whose future are not threatened by oppression of either the Government or other things.

(ii) People whose environment is characterized with peace are often contended people, especially when they consider the price of conflicts and wars. More often than not, people go into war when their lives, peace or freedom are under attack or serious threats.

(iii) The peace in the nation can bring about stability in the political, economic and social set-ups and infrastructures. People tend to feel so insecure when their peace are under threats. Insecurities make some people to behave in some irrational ways, including taking laws into their hands. When they go that far, civil unrest or even war is in the making. People only know when a war begins, they do not know when it will end and no one knows what it will cost the nation in terms of lives and properties.

Nigeria May Be Blessed: This line of the old national anthem recognizes the fact that the country can only be truly blessed if everybody identifies his or her roles and plays it accordingly. The followings are the expected roles to be played by all Nigerians before they can be truly blessed by God of creation whom they believe, going by the old and the new national anthems:

(1) The cause of the nation must be appreciated and respected through deeds and what is taught everywhere in Nigeria, including schools.

(2) All Nigerians must see all the land as their native land without giving any room for ethnic strife, which can result into division. Division is the mother of conflicts, which can grow into war. A Nigerian from the North can claim to be from or can be born in the South and vice versa.

(3) No matter their differences either in languages or tribes, they must see themselves as brothers and sisters. If they see themselves as the same family, they will feel the need to keep and protect one another against enemies from outside the country since a country that is divided against itself cannot stand.

(4) Nigerians must be ready and proud to serve Nigeria which is their sovereign motherland.

(5) With the flag which symbolizes peace and abundance, all Nigerians must always stand together for truth and justice and be ready to embed the same in the minds of their children instead of considering one another as enemies. By considering themselves as enemies, they work against the interests, the future and the unity of the nation.

These Children Are Probably Born Under Oppressive Government In The Nation That Is Characterized With Hunger And Sufferings. Their Parents Are Probably Those Who Did Nothing About The Future Of The Children Before They Were Born

(6) Nigerians must be ready to sacrifice anything for the peace of their country and then expect honour

through the act of sacrifice.

(7) Nigerians must be ready to hand over good legacy to their children, who in turn must be ready to hand over the same good legacy like a banner without stain to their own children when they become adults

(8) With the help of God, Nigerians must be ready to build the nation through their contributions into the economy, politics, welfare, education and other things that will make life meaningful to others.

(9) No Nigerian must feel superior or inferior to others because these two complexities can make one the oppressor and the other the oppressed. Any slightest trace of oppression can serve as bacteria that threaten the entire body of the nation.

(10) Finally, all Nigerians must strive to be at peace with everybody, including other Nigerians that act as enemies. This may prove to be a little difficult but where there is a will, there is a way.

The above are the analysis of the old national anthem and its comparison with the new anthem. Let us now study the new national anthem.

THE NEW NATIONAL ANTHEM

The new national anthem of Nigeria was adopted in 1978. Unlike the old anthem, the lyrics are not composed by one person. Wordings of the new national anthem are combinations of words and phrases taken from five of the best entries in a nation contest. The lyrics are composed into a music by the Nigerian Police Band under the directorship of Benedict E. Odiase while the lyrics are extracted from the entries of John A. Ilechukwu, Eme Etim Akpan, B. A Ogunnaike, Sota Omoigui and P.O Aderibigbe.

The analysis of the new national anthem is one of the proofs that there are fine poets in Nigeria. It also indicates that two good heads are truly better than one good head. Having five good heads to come up with the new national anthem is indeed a great contribution to the Nigeria Value System, going by the analysis.

The new national anthem goes thus:

Arise, o compatriots,
Nigerian's call obey
To serve our fatherland
With love and strength and faith
The labour of our heroes' past
Shall never be in vain
To serve with heart and might
One nation bound in freedom,
Peace and unity

Oh God of creation,
Direct our noble cause
Guide our leaders right
Help our youths the truth to know
In love and honesty to grow
And living just and true
Great lofty heights attain
To build the nation where peace
And justice shall reign

THE ANALYSIS OF THE NEW NATIONAL ANTHEM:

Arise, O Compatriots: The first line begins with someone who seems to call the attentions of the citizens (compatriots) to the tasks ahead of them. Citizens whose attentions are called this way probably need to be informed of the things which may be of national interests either because they are unconscious of them or oblivious of the implications of neglecting them. By asking all citizens to "arise", the line tries to wake Nigerians up or make them meet up to their responsibilities as citizens.

Nigeria's Call Obey: This line reveals the identity of the person that calls as the nation of Nigeria. In essence, the nation assumes the position of authority. With this authority, everybody is expected to obey the call without hesitation like in the army, especially when it is for important or urgent purposes or both. This call, in whichever way it comes, must be obeyed. This call applies to all citizens, not only the Nigerian soldiers. Sometimes it comes through the children who count on adults to protect them from danger. If the person does not obey the call, it can amount into a crime. Thus, both Criminal and Civil laws indicate that an omission or commission can constitute an offence or a crime. For instance, a man who sees a child taking poison which the man knows can kill him would be held responsible for whatever happens to the child if he does not stop him from taking it. Nigeria's call to be obeyed are in the following ways:

1. All Nigerians are mandated to carry out their civic duties and responsibilities such as reporting any criminal activity around them to the police or doing all they can to help those who are in danger.

2. All Nigerians are mandated to abide by the law, including State and Federal laws. They are also mandated to abide by the rules and order within their communities or organizations where they work or institutions or schools where they are students or in other places that are legally constituted. Violation of any State or Federal laws often constitutes a crime which the State Prosecutor can prosecute.

3. All Nigerians are also mandated not to give room for offence against each other such as breach of contract and others that are actionable under either Contract, Marriage and or other laws.

To Serve Our Fatherland: Although this line seems to be woven with the next line of the anthem but the services to the fatherland called Nigeria has more than what it seems. Thus the services to Nigeria include though not limited to the followings:

(1) Complete obedience to the law of fatherland, including Constitutional, Criminal and other laws.

(2) Serving the nation through one way or the other as may be demanded by the law such the National Youth Service Corps who sometimes are called to assist in the electoral process of electing leaders.

(3) Serving the nation through community development or by educating other citizens of things of national interests. Since no Government in the world can meet all the needs of its people, citizens are needed to contribute in cash or kind into the society for the good of others.

With Love And Strength And Faith: Just as in the pledge to Nigeria which is meant to characterize Nigerians to be faithful; loyal and honest people, this line of the national anthem aims at making them to be loving, full of strength and

23

faith. The followings depict the attributes that are intended by this line:

(i) _Love_: This is the greatest of all characteristics in a person. Love is usually a two-way street that exists between two or more people. Love is what brings two persons together and raise a family. Love is what keep the family members together. It is the same love that keeps families together as a community. Love keeps the communities that constitute a state or nation together as one. This love of the fatherland must not be compromised if the country is to survive as a nation. A nation that is devoid of love cannot stand because it would be characterized with hatred and malice which give births to struggles and battles. It is love of the fatherland that made so many soldiers to die during the civil war that broke out in 1967. Love is not just in what people say but also in what they do and what they are ready to sacrifice.

(ii) _Strength_: It is love of something or someone that gives people the strength to get that thing that is loved or to make sacrifices for the loved ones. If fallen heroes did not love their fatherland, where would they get the strength to fight for the unity of Nigeria? Strength which the anthem is trying to depict is in the following terms: (a) Serving the nation with passion and determination (b) serving the nation sacrificially with whatever is available and (C) serving the nation without expecting anything in return but with the hope that others would benefit from the sacrifice. Nigeria is still united today because some people paid the sacrifices to keep it united.

(iii) _Faith_: This line would be explained in the pledge to Nigeria but it is worthy to note that many people become criminals today, not because they want to constitute problems to the nation. They become criminals because they lost their faith either in the leaders or their parents or the nation as a whole. What all Nigerians must understand is the rationale behind what Edmund Burke said, which is: _the only thing necessary for the triumph of evils is for good people to do nothing._ In other words, if good people do not love their country to the extent of sacrificing all they can so as to secure the future, the evil that men do will not only live after their deaths but can also destroy every good thing others have achieved, thereby creating a society of evil citizens.

The Labour Of Our Heroes' Past: This line reminds Nigerians of those who have sacrificed so much, including their lives so that the citizens will enjoy the peace in the country. Any nation that had been through civil war will understand what it costs to fight battles. Thus there is need to study the history of Nigeria so as to appreciate the sacrifices of the past heroes. They will also understand the mistakes of past leaders and be well informed about their country. "The labour of our heroes' past" can be depicted in terms of the heroes' tussle over the wealth of the nation, the struggle to keep it save, the battle to make citizens be at peace with one another and to keep the unity of Nigeria.

Shall Never Be In Vain: This line is aimed at reminding Nigerians that the tussles, the struggles and the battles of the past heroes must not be allowed to be in vain. All these heroes in the past are either dead or too old or invalid to do anything again. In other words, they have given all they could and these sacrifices must not be in vain.

To Serve With Heart And Might: This line challenges all Nigerians to serve their nation with hearts and might since this is what the past heroes did, going by the history of the civil war. Unless Nigerians love their fatherland; which gives them strength and faith in Nigeria, they may not be able to serve with their hearts and might. Serving with heart is synonymous with passion to serve while might is using available material resources, talents; physical and mental abilities of the citizens. Any Nigerian who uses his or her position or the available resources to serve his or her interest is not serving the nation. Anyone who uses his or her resources, including talents or position to incite or mislead the people either through entertainments or education or other methods, thereby encouraging social vices breaks the law. He maybe found guilty as the offenders.

One Nation Bound In Freedom: This line makes it clear that if every Nigerian selflessly serves the nation with heart and might, the society will be free. A nation that is bound in freedom will have its citizens free from the followings:

(i) Freedom from dictatorship type of Government or Colonial masters.

(ii) Freedom from conflicts of interests, especially the one that can result into tussles of powers or struggles for freedom or battles like civil wars.

(iii) Freedom from social vices and crimes which often pose threats to lives and properties, creating security challenges.

Peace And Unity: Although this aspect had been explained in the old anthem but it is instructive to note that the peace and unity of any nation has their price tags, going by historical backgrounds of many nations, including Nigeria. Without making the necessary sacrifices, peace and unity is nearly impossible. The reason is that there are many things that can threaten the peace and unity of a nation. The commonest of those things are as follow:

(i) By nature, man often seeks power to control. Everybody wants to be in charge of everything, especially what concerns him or her. Both parents want to control each other and their children. Their children also want to control their parents and teachers. Government wants to control citizens while people want to control the Government. So most people seek the power to control, including going diabolical. The laws, therefore, are enacted to regulate the conduct of everybody, including the leaders.

(ii) When most leaders get to the positions of authority either through force or electoral or other means, they often times disregard what the law says. Some go as far as trying to change what the law says in order to remain in power. This kind of attitude is a serious threat to the peace and unity of the nation.

(iii) Another threat is sometimes caused by ignorance or negligence or arrogance of some leaders who are unfit to navigate the collective efforts of the citizens to the "noble cause". When the citizens, especially the radicals among them see this weakness of the leaders, they begin to incite the people against the Government mostly with the objective of getting the power to control. This often leads to rebellion that threatens the peace and unity of the nation.

(iv) Another threats to peace and unity of the nation are vices and crimes. All nations in the world are vulnerable to vices and crimes. The reasons includes the fact that while some people use societal vices and crimes to enrich themselves or gain power, others are simply sadistic enough to enjoy them, such as rapists. For the sake of peace and unity, the laws are enacted to regulate conduct of citizens and sanction anyone who breaks any of them.

Oh God Of Creation: Unlike the national anthems in some countries, this line of the second stanza indicates that Nigeria as a nation officially recognizes the belief in God and acknowledges him as the creator of creations. This aspect of belief in God also reflects in the old anthem and in the pledge to Nigeria as would be explained later.

Direct Our Noble Cause: With the belief in God, this line encourages Nigerians to always ask God for direction in their collective efforts towards the noble cause which includes, but not limited to the followings:

1. The quest to bake the national cake for the good of old, young and future generation with everyone getting his or her fair share as it is explained in the introduction of the book.
2. To help in the healing process of the fatherland which is infected with deadly bacteria which can be considered as vices and crimes in the society. These bacteria are deadly enough to either knock down the whole system in the country or destroy it completely.
3. To pursue peace and unity of the nation as indicated in the pledge to Nigeria. This encourages citizens to be their brothers' keepers, or to seek for leadership positions with the aim to serve the people and not to be served.
4. To fulfill the promises which all citizens have made to the nation through the pledge to Nigeria at any point of their lives.

Guide Our Leaders Right: This line recognizes the need to pray for leaders because, more often than not, they are the authors of tales of woes of every nation. When the head is good, other parts of the body will perform well. If it is bad, every part may malfunction. The reasons leaders need to be by guided by God, going by historical facts are as follow:

1. Leaders are human being just like the citizens. Thus they are prone of human errors. Human error sometimes affect the generations yet unborn as it is experienced in Nigeria where the wealth of the nation was mismanaged and made indebted to other nations through loans, which extend from one generation to another. Thomas Jefferson said, *"loading up the nation with debts and leaving it for the following generations to pay is morally irresponsible. Excessive debt*

is a means by which governments oppress the people and waste their substance. No nation has a right to contract debt for periods longer than the majority contracting it can expect to live."

2. Leaders need guidance of God in decision making, especially the one that involves going into war with another country. Making wrong decisions have cost the wealth of some countries and millions of lives of citizens of many nations as in the case of second world war.

3. Other reasons the nation needs God's guidance also include safeguarding the lives of the leaders. As it is observed in Nigeria, some good Governments are not always given chance to build the nation as they desired before ambitious and selfish people overthrow them. Bad government, however, often seems to know how to remain in power for a very long time. The more bad government remains in power, the more good things are destroyed and replaced with bad things.

Help Our Youth The Truth To Know: This line is a prayer to God and also a recognition of the fact that without truth, youth may see good things as bad, bad things as good. Without truth, innocent people may look like criminals while criminals will look innocent. Without truth, those who are supposed to be looked up behind bars would be celebrated and sometimes given chieftaincy and religious titles. Without truth, youths may sacrifice their future for the present gains. Truths which youths need to know about their countries, include but not limited to the followings:

(i) Most people, including their leaders all over the world often live by lies; deceptions and manipulations. Although it must be admitted that there are things that need to be kept secret but most of the things that are concealed in secrecy are supposed to be revealed to the public. It is truth that reveals the true identities of those who are to be chosen to lead in any area of life, including business, politics and religion.

(ii) It is truth that empowers everybody, especially the youths who can easily be deceived and used by other people to achieve their illicit or evil desires. Many youths are made to be involved in things that can destroy them, going by results of various research works. Most inmates in Nigerian prisons are youths or middle aged people who have wasted their youthful periods and available resources instead of them to contribute them into the "noble cause" of the nation. If they had known the truth about their conduct, according to those who were interviewed, they would not get involved in what would land them in prisons.

(iii) Youths also need to know the truth so that their lives and that of their children in future can be protected. Obviously, if youths are ignorance of the truth about basic things about life, they will constitute nuisance instead of being relevant in the society. A lot of Nigerian youths in modern days had been lured by those they befriend to places they were used as ritual sacrifices. These who do not know the implication of such crimes often grow into terrorists as it is common in the society.

And Living Just And True: This line of the anthem is also a request to God to make Nigerian youths to live just and true life. It also recognizes the fact that the knowledge of the truth in the preceding line (Help Our Youth The Truth To Know) that helps to live just and true life. The word "just" can be explained as being moral, responsible and reasonable. While the word "true" in this context means real. Thus this line can be explained in line with the previous lines, saying that God should help Nigerian youths to understand that the real life of a Nigerian must be lived in moral, reasonable and responsible ways. Apart from knowing the truth, other things that can help youth to live just and true life include the followings:

(i) *The fear of God*. This makes a person God-fearing. Going by histories of various countries that had been studied, nations which do not officially recognize the belief in God is vulnerable to vices and crimes. For this reason a Russian dictator called Vladimir Lenin who can be rightly considered as the person responsible for the deaths of tens of millions of people said that the best revolution are youths devoid of morals. To make a person devoid of morals is to remove every fear or belief in God. History indicates that anyone who does not fear God can be very dangerous in the society.

(ii) *The love for humanity*: This is also important in making the people to live just and true life. As Karl Marx once observed when he said *"religion is the opium of the people"*, the belief in the gods that demand for blood of fellow human beings can be used to cause catastrophe in the society. The love for humanity, however, can counter such belief and possibly make them understand that "God Of Creation" will never instruct anyone to destroy his work, let alone to kill fellow human beings for whatever reasons. In other words, the love for humanity will hold the notion that *"you do to others what you would have them to do to you."*

(iii) *The Belief In The Value System:* This system which is embedded in the national anthem and the pledge to Nigeria is enforced by the laws, making citizens live just and true. If youths are conscious of the fact that all their actions either good or bad have consequences, they will live right. From the interviews the author of this book have conducted with some inmates in different prisons in Nigeria, most of them either do not know nor believe that their conduct will land them in jail. While vast majority of youths are not educated of Nigerian value system by their teachers, some do not even know about the value system. Others who know about it deliberately violate it because of the incentives they find in vices and crimes. When they are faced with the consequences of their actions, they begin to look for people like their parents and government to blame.

Great Lofty Heights Attain: This line is also a request to God Of Creation, praying that through the youths, Nigeria will attain great and lofty heights, which connotes great achievements in various walks of life such as Medicine; Engineering, Law, Politics, Education, Humanity, Character Building professions and other areas. However, there is no way anyone can attain any of these heights without following these basic principles, which can be studied in one of the author's books titled "Building Your Future And The Nation Now".

1. Youths must appreciate the value of time. In other words, they need to understand that they must spend time to enhance their value in life by getting educated or starting to acquire experiences in their chosen careers instead

Moving Up On The Ladder Of Life May Not Be An Easy Task But The Youth Who Patiently Takes One Step After The Other Will Easily Move Up

of wasting it on pleasures. Any of their hours that is wasted is a part of their lives that is wasted, which may not be recovered.

2. They must not give up in their efforts to achieve great things in life, knowing fully well that there are many others, including their families that would benefit from their efforts.

3. They must never be lazy. Any lazy person cannot go beyond the ground level of the "Great Lofty Heights".

4. They must live a simple life instead of complicated or double life.

5. They must be honest in their dealings, according to the pledge they make to Nigeria. A dishonest person is either a nuisance in the society or a rogue that stains the names of his or her family, community and the nation.

6. They must be kind to fellow citizens so that they may also receive the same treatment. Human beings are usually the reflections of whom we are in the inside. As a kind person often seems to be surrounded by kind persons, wicked people often seem surrounded by wicked people. That is the reason the adage says a murderer would not give room for anyone to play with sword around him. The reason, of course, is that he is always suspicious that someone maybe planning to kill him just as has killed others.

7. Youths must never shun their responsibilities and duties to the nation, their families and fellow citizens.

8. They must be judicious in their spending. Since they are still depending on other people, every amount of money they get must be invested in themselves or their future such as building their careers or getting trained in their chosen professions.

9. To attain a great and lofty heights in life, it takes time and lots of efforts. So youths who want to reach the peak of their careers in life must be very patient. Those who tries to take short cuts always shortens their successes and most times their lives. This accounts for the rate at which youths of nowadays are losing their lives. The outcome of research works indicates that impatience often makes youths to cut corners, making them to either end up in prisons or lose their lives.

10. Finally, youths must always acquire and improve on their skills. Through that, they enhance their value in life.

To Build A Nation: When youths of any society makes efforts to enhance their value in life by following the above principles, the nation will be well built

One Of The Best Ways To Build A Nation Is To Build The Children. Children That Are Not Built Will Either Become Destitute Or Threats To Lives And Properties

on a solid foundation. If the youths do not build themselves, they will destroy the existing infrastructures to build the economy, political and other systems in the society. According to the book: "Building Your future And The Nation Now," the wealth of a nation is not in its financial, natural or other

Kidnappers That Hold Expatriates To A Ransom - Part Of The Proofs Of The Near Extinction Of The Nigerian Value System

resources but rather in the attitudes of the citizens of the country. In other words, attitudes of the citizens are either the assets that bring blessings or burdens that brings pains and sorrow to the nation. For this reason, one of the American greatest Presidents, John Kennedy told American citizens when their country was faced with challenges, *"think of what you can do for your country, not what the country will do for you."* Citizens do not build a nation by placing demand on the nation. Thus youths need to think of how to build the nation by making efforts to build themselves into responsible, reasonable and successful members who allows other citizens to benefit from their efforts. When they do this, they will earn the respects of members of the society who can elect them as their leaders.

Where Peace And Justice Shall Reign: This line emphasizes the fact that peace and justice can only reign when the above steps are taken and the pledges that are made to Nigeria are fulfilled. The point in this line is explained in the old anthem under the headings of: "That Truth And Justice Reign" and "In Peace Or Battle honoured"

Having explained the new national anthem, which proves to

be far better than the old, it is also vital to explain the pledge to Nigeria so that every Nigerian may understand the implication of breaking any of them.

THE PLEDGE TO NIGERIA

I Pledge To Nigeria, My Country: This pledge is very crucial for all Nigerians to make to the nation because it makes them very conscious of what the law says as it reflects in the national anthem, making them obedient and committed to the society at the early stages of their lives.

To Be Faithful, Loyal And Honest: These three great virtues need to characterize every Nigerian who at least passes through Primary School because most, if not all of them would one day become either Family Heads or Community or Political or other Leaders in future:

(I) *Faithfulness*: This is meant to characterize Nigerians as faithful people who believe in the cause and purpose of the nation, making them responsible and law-abiding citizens. It is also important for all Nigerians to be faithful, especially in the things that are of national interest because unfaithfulness gives room for malpractice that ranges from cheating during examination to electoral fraud. Any act of unfaithfulness is a violation of this pledge, which can amount to a crime.

(II) *Loyalty*: This attribute needs to be embedded in all Nigerians because history indicates that the levels of loyalties of the citizens of every society are often tested in the time of crisis, where sometimes people are tempted to allow personal interests to take precedence over national interest. By and large, the pledge makes disloyalty to the nation an outright betrayal which can amount to Felony or Treason like cases of coup d'etat which set Nigeria backward.

(III) *Honesty*: This aspect of The Pledge To Nigeria is meant to teach all Nigerians to be honest in all their dealings either in politics or business or other things. Any act of dishonesty in a society or organization or institution can cause a stain in the reputation of the people within. There was a time when

Nigerians who were applying for visas to other countries would have to prove that they not fraudulent because they are not trusted. The Police, Civil Servants and other people were assumed to be dishonest by other countries because of fraudulent practice that was common till now. The author of this book had the experience of how a stain in the reputation of the nation could feel like when his book was about to be published in USA. The publishers wanted him to prove it to them that he is the owner of the intellectual property that was submitted to them for publication. The reason, according to them, was that the US Government back then have warned them to be very careful in the way they dealt with Nigerians. This so provoked the author that he told them that he would rather prove it to them that there were more criminals in US than in Nigeria than to prove that he is the author. He cancelled the deal with the publishers.

To Serve Nigeria With All My Strength: This line implies the total commitments of all Nigerians to the good of the nation by carrying out their duties and responsibilities in this order of priority:

(a) To The Nation
(b) To Their Families and
(c) To Fellow Nigerians.

If this order is misplaced, there would be conflicts of interests, which can result into chain of reactions, including divisions. Divisions can cause conflicts, which can result into breaking the law.

To Defend Her Unity: This line is a cord that holds all Nigerians together despite their differences in languages, customs, religions and lifestyles. Without the mind to defend the unity of Nigeria, there would be conflicts and divisions like the one that almost caused the nation to break into different countries during the civil war. To defend the unity of Nigeria, the people must never dwell on the differences in their interests, religions, cultures, lifestyles and other things. They should dwell on common grounds like the constitution that guarantees every Nigerian's fundamental human rights.

Uphold Her Honour And Glory: It is honourable attitude that brings glory to a nation. Dishonourable attitudes of Nigerians, especially political, religious and other leaders bring shame and dishonour to the country. Upholding the honour and glory of any country lies in the patriotic attitudes of both leaders and the citizens of Nigeria.

<u>So Help Me God</u>: This line just as it is indicated and explained in both old and new national anthems, recognizes the fact that there are forms of beliefs in God in virtually all norms and cultures that constitute the Nigerian Value System. Invariably, this line of The Pledge makes most Nigerians believe there is God and this may characterize them as religious people. Although Karl Marx may seem to be right when he said, "religion is the opium of the people," especially if we consider how it had been used to cause crises in Nigeria, but if we study the horrifying effects of a nation that never officially believe in God as influenced by people like Karl Marx and Lenin, we would conclude that a Godless nation is vulnerable to all sorts of crimes and evils, including terrorism. Theories of such people have created more catastrophes in the history of man than anything good as it is observed in some countries like Russia where dictators like Lenin and Stalin caused the deaths of tens of millions of people. While building on Karl Marx theories, Lenin said that the best revolutionists are youths devoid of morals. Going by the study of his activities and that of his successor, Stalin, revolutionists were people whose ideas agreed with theirs though they may be murderous while their enemies were those who disagreed with them in any way. This is what accounted for the mass murder of millions of Russians.

Religion, however, can truly become opium of the people if it is not made voluntary by reasons or logics. However good a religion may seem to be, if it is enforced on the people either by coercion or manipulation, it will amount to an attack on their freewill and may also violate their fundamental human right of choice of religion as guaranteed by the constitution. The end result is rebellion which may lead to conflicts or breaking of the law. The belief in God which needs to be influenced by reasons and logics instead of being enforced, plays the following roles in the nation:

I. It boosts the moral values of the people by making them feel that there is God who pays everyone, according to his or her deeds, whether good or bad.

II. Because God is perceived as being capable of bringing judgment upon the people who violate any of his commandments, the belief in God makes them God-fearing. God-fearing people are law-abiding people.

III. Among other things, belief in God can bring peace, tolerance, joy and harmony within the society.

Any religion which does not play all the above roles must not be encouraged in the society. All religions or groups which pose threats to human lives or properties needs to be wiped out since they contravene the law and order.

Apart from giving the students the picture of Nigerian Value System, the anthems and the pledge are ways of making them to master what the law says as indicated.

CONCLUSION WITH THE STORY OF THE FOUR YOUNG COMPATRIOTS WHO MAKE NIGERIA GREAT

There were four young Compatriots called Promise, Faithful, Loyal and Honest who came from the Eastern, Western, Southern and Northern parts of Nigeria.

When they were in schools, they were made to pledge to serve the nation with all their strengths; to defend her unity; uphold her honour and glory. They knew, however, that they cannot fulfil these pledges without the help of God because of their limitations as youths back then. So they always pray to God to help them.

They were taught in the school of the National Values where they realized that failures to keep the pledge they made to Nigeria can result into vices or crimes which can take them to jail or even cause them to lose their lives. They were also made to understand that they were the future of the nation and whatever they did at their young age would determine if they would be useful or useless to their families, communities and the nation at large. If they were disciplined; well-equipped and informed for the future, they stand the chances of becoming great leaders in the fields of politics, business, medicine, education and other aspects of life.

With these in mind, they aspired to be the best they could by making best use of the opportunities and resources that were made available either by the Government or their families or other people who were willing to support them in their chosen careers.

While they worked hard to fulfil these pledges and enhance their value in life, so many other youths who can be called

Indiscipline, Unruly, Heady, Ignorant, Carefree, Selfish, Malicious and Ferocious were busy breaking the pledges they also made to Nigeria. The four young compatriots refused to join the company of these other youths since their conduct indicated that they were going through the direction that is different from the noble cause. Also through the violation of the pledge to the nation, it was apparent to them that the bad gang will soon end up their lives either in prisons or graves.

As part of their services to the nation, the young Compatriots tried to positively influence the bad gang to be of good behaviour. Some of them changed their ways and joined the good company of Compatriots while the rest form vice rings like secret cults, group of terrorists, fraudsters and other agents of societal problems.

Soon enough, Nigerian fatherland which was once peaceful became hostile environment where lives and potentials were either threatened or destroyed. Armed-robberies, sales of parts of human bodies and human trafficking became rampant in the society. The system began to go down with only few trying to bring it back to work. These vices and crimes began to destroy the economic and the political structures, making most people either threatened, sick or tired of living.

The madness in the fatherland of Nigerians spread round the nation. This compelled some people to fly out and become third class citizens or illegal immigrants in another country. Many others who cannot leave the country are forced to apply any means to survive, including killing others for money or using their children to steal or flirt around like street dogs.

Still these four Compatriots refused to give up their faith in God of creation who gave them strength to sail through the ocean of insanity. Because they love their country, they made lots of sacrifices for her in spite of the fact that they also needed help. They shared their things with other Compatriots who do not have the strength to hang on during this period of crisis. They educated others of the need to be on the side of God.

These Compatriots continued to pray for everybody, including the leaders who seemed confused by what is happening, saying:

"Oh God of creation,

Direct our noble cause
Guide our leaders right
Help our youths the truth to know
In love and honesty to grow
And living just and true
Great lofty heights attain
To build the nation where peace
And justice shall reign"

Because of this prayer and because they refused to go crazy like many other people who do crazy things, God begins to prepare them to become responsible leaders about twenty years later.

God later used these Compatriots to remove the madness in Nigeria while members of the bad company are either dead as a result of their involvement in vices or crimes or became destitute people or others that spend their productive lives in prisons.

This is the true picture of Nigeria and destinies of young Nigerians.

Nigerians can now decide their future and that of the nation. The decision is not in what they say and think alone but also in what they do.

All young Nigerians have the chance of making their country a better place to stay or leave their destinies in the hands of those who are ready to destroy them.

The final question is: What Is Your Decision? You have to give the final answer. If you have decided to be one of the young Compatriots that would make Nigeria great, you can take another step by reading another of the author's book titled: Building Your Future And The Nation Now.

www.ingramcontent.com/pod-product-compliance
Lightning Source LLC
Chambersburg PA
CBHW060704280326
41933CB00012B/2302